LE CORDON BLEU

HOME COLLECTION

·SAUCES·

D0537597

MEREHURST

contents

recipe ratings ✦ *easy* ✦✦ *a little more care needed* ✦✦✦ *more care needed*

White wine sauce

This elegant sauce is shown here with poached white fish and vegetables.

*Preparation time **10 minutes***
*Total cooking time **40 minutes***
Makes approximately 300 ml (10 fl oz)

15 g (¹/₂ oz) unsalted butter
3 French shallots, finely chopped
300 ml (10 fl oz) white wine
300 ml (10 fl oz) chicken or fish stock (see page 61)
400 ml (12³/4 fl oz) thick (double) cream

1 Melt the butter in a heavy-based pan over low heat. Gently cook the shallots in the pan, without colouring, until they are soft and transparent.

2 Pour in the white wine, scraping the base of the pan with a wooden spoon. Turn up the heat and boil until the liquid has reduced by half. Add the stock and boil until the liquid has reduced to 100 ml (3¹/4 fl oz).

3 Stir in the cream and continue to reduce the sauce until it is thick enough to coat the back of a spoon.

4 Pass the sauce through a fine sieve if you wish. Season, to taste, with salt and pepper. Serve warm. It may be kept warm over a pan of simmering water for up to half an hour before serving. Do not allow the water to boil at this stage or the saucce may split. This sauce goes best with fish or chicken.

Chef's tips Use a stock to complement the dish with which you serve it, for example, a chicken stock for chicken dishes.

To prevent a skin forming on this sauce while keeping hot, cover the surface with plastic wrap.

Green peppercorn sauce

This pungent peppery sauce, laced with brandy, is pictured with steak and new potatoes.

*Preparation time **10 minutes***
*Total cooking time **15 minutes***
Makes approximately 200 ml (6¹/2 fl oz)

30 g (1 oz) green peppercorns, drained
100 ml (3¹/4 oz) brandy
300 ml (10 fl oz) brown or lamb stock (see page 60)
100 ml (3¹/4 fl oz) thick (double) cream

1 Place the peppercorns in a heavy-based pan and, at a very low heat, warm through for 1–2 minutes, until dry, being careful not to burn them. Roughly break the peppercorns against the sides of the pan using the back of a wooden spoon.

2 Pour the brandy into the pan, turn up the heat and quickly boil for 1–2 minutes, or until the brandy has evaporated. Stir in the stock, bring to the boil and boil for about 5 minutes, or until the liquid has reduced by one quarter.

3 Add the cream and continue to reduce over high heat until the sauce coats the back of the spoon. Season, to taste, with salt, and pepper if required. Serve immediately, with juicy grilled or pan-fried red meat such as steak or chops.

Chef's tip This sauce has quite a strong peppery taste because the green peppercorns are cooked in the sauce from the beginning. If you want instead a burst of flavour from each individual peppercorn, proceed with steps 1 and 2 up to evaporating the brandy. In a separate pan, reduce the stock and cream, then add to the peppercorns and brandy. Stir and season to taste.

White wine sauce (top) and Green peppercorn sauce

Creamy mushroom sauce

Button mushrooms lend a mild, earthy flavour to this sauce, which we have shown with chargrilled fillet steak, steamed baby zucchini and carrots.

Preparation time **15 minutes**
Total cooking time **15 minutes**
Makes approximately 400 ml (13 fl oz)

60 g (2 oz) unsalted butter
4 large French shallots, finely chopped
200 g (6 1/2 oz) button mushrooms, finely chopped
leaves from 1 stem of fresh tarragon
100 ml (3 1/4 fl oz) white wine
600 ml (20 fl oz) brown stock (see page 60)
2 tablespoons cream or sour cream

1 Melt the butter over low heat in a frying pan. Add the shallots and cook for 2 minutes, or until soft and transparent, without colouring. Increase the heat, add the mushrooms and tarragon and cook for 5–7 minutes, or until the mushrooms are golden brown. The mushrooms will make their own liquid. Cook until this has evaporated and they are dry.

2 Pour in the white wine, scraping the bottom of the pan with a wooden spoon to lift off the sticky sediment that contains a lot of flavour. Add the stock and boil until it has reduced by half. Season, to taste, with salt and pepper. Strain and transfer the mushroooms to a food processor or blender and blend until smooth. Add the stock, a couple of tablespoons at a time, then add the cream and blend to combine. Transfer to a pan to reheat as necessary. To serve, pour the sauce into a warmed sauce boat, spoon onto the base of a plate and serve the food on top or spoon over the food. Serve with grilled meat or poached white fish or chicken.

Mustard sauce

This is a smooth, piquant sauce perfect to serve with rabbit, veal or pork. We have shown it with veal nut and roast potatoes.

Preparation time **10 minutes**
Total cooking time **20 minutes**
Makes approximately 250 ml (8 fl oz)

20 g (3/4 oz) unsalted butter
1 large French shallot, finely chopped
100 ml (3 1/4 fl oz) white wine
300 ml (10 fl oz) brown stock (see page 60)
50 ml (1 3/4 fl oz) thick (double) cream
1 1/2 tablespoons Dijon mustard

1 Melt the butter in a saucepan over low heat, add the shallot and cook gently, without colouring, until soft and transparent.

2 Pour in the wine, scraping the base of the pan with a wooden spoon to lift and blend in the flavourful sediment. Stir in the stock, bring to the boil and then reduce the heat to a simmer. Boil, uncovered, until the liquid has reduced by half. Stir in the cream, simmer for another 2–3 minutes and then strain the sauce through a fine sieve into a clean pan.

3 Whisk in the Dijon mustard and season, to taste, with salt and pepper. Reheat gently to serve.

White sauce

Create a variety of sauces by adding flavours to this basic sauce, pictured here with broccoli and cauliflower. See page 62 for step-by-step instructions to accompany this recipe.

*Preparation time **5 minutes***
*Total cooking time **10 minutes***
*Makes approximately **550 ml (18 fl oz)***

30 g (1 oz) unsalted butter
30 g (1 oz) plain flour
500 ml (16 fl oz) milk
small pinch of ground nutmeg

1 Melt the butter in a heavy-based pan over low-medium heat. Sprinkle the flour over the butter and cook for 1–2 minutes without allowing it to colour, stirring continuously with a wooden spoon.
2 Remove the pan from the heat and slowly add the milk, whisking to avoid lumps. Return to medium heat and bring to the boil, stirring constantly. Cook for 3–4 minutes, or until the sauce coats the back of a spoon. If the sauce has lumps, pass it through a fine sieve and reheat in a clean pan. Season with salt, pepper and nutmeg. Serve hot.

Chef's tip Flavour the sauce by adding an onion studded with cloves to the milk, then warming the milk through.

Mornay sauce

A white sauce enriched with cheese and egg yolks makes a perfect topping for the scallops shown here. To finish, simply flash under the grill until golden brown.

*Preparation time **10 minutes***
*Total cooking time **15 minutes***
*Makes approximately **550 ml (18 fl oz)***

30 g (1 oz) unsalted butter
30 g (1 oz) plain flour
500 ml (16 fl oz) milk
2 egg yolks
100 g (3¼ oz) Gruyère cheese, grated
pinch of ground nutmeg

1 Melt the butter in a heavy-based pan over low-medium heat. Sprinkle the flour over the butter and cook for 1–2 minutes without allowing it to colour, stirring continuously with a wooden spoon.
2 Remove the pan from the heat and slowly add the milk, whisking to avoid lumps. Return to medium heat and bring to the boil, stirring constantly. Cook for 3–4 minutes, or until the sauce coats the back of a spoon. If the sauce has lumps, pass it through a fine sieve and reheat in a clean pan.
3 Remove from the stove, add the yolks and cheese off the heat and mix. Season with salt, pepper and nutmeg.

White sauce (top) and Mornay sauce

Suprême sauce

This creamy velouté sauce is the accompaniment to the classic poached chicken dish, Chicken suprême. It is also delicious, however, with grilled chicken breast as shown here.

Preparation time **5 minutes**
Total cooking time **15 minutes**
Makes approximately 800 ml (26 fl oz)

40 g (1¼ oz) unsalted butter
40 g (1¼ oz) plain flour
450 ml (14¼ fl oz) hot chicken stock (see page 61)
400 ml (12¾ fl oz) thick (double) cream
50 g (1¾ oz) unsalted butter, cubed, optional

1 Melt the butter in a deep heavy-based pan over low-medium heat. Sprinkle the flour over the butter and cook for 1–2 minutes without allowing it to colour, stirring continuously with a wooden spoon. The mixture should be white and frothy. Remove from the heat. Stir in a little hot stock and blend well using a wooden spoon or whisk. Little by little, add the remaining stock.
2 Return to the heat and whisk to avoid lumps as you slowly bring the sauce to the boil. Lower the heat and gently simmer for 3–4 minutes, stirring or whisking continuously. Stir in the cream and continue to simmer for 2–3 minutes, or until the sauce coats the back of a spoon. If the sauce has lumps, pass it through a fine sieve and reheat in a clean pan. Season with salt and white pepper. To add extra shine, whisk in the cubed butter. Serve this sauce immediately.

Caper sauce

Traditionally served with boiled leg of lamb, this sauce with its sharp, piquant taste of capers is also excellent with roast loin of lamb and vegetables as shown.

Preparation time **15 minutes**
Total cooking time **45 minutes**
Makes approximately 500 ml (16 fl oz)

30 g (1 oz) unsalted butter
30 g (1 oz) plain flour
500 ml (16 fl oz) hot lamb stock (see page 60)
2 egg yolks
50 ml (1¾ fl oz) thick (double) cream
60 g (2 oz) capers, drained and chopped

1 Melt the butter in a medium-sized, deep heavy-based pan over low-medium heat. Sprinkle the flour over the butter, mix in and cook gently, stirring continuously, until the mixture is lightly golden. Remove from the heat.
2 Stir in a little hot stock and blend well using a wooden spoon or whisk. Return to the heat and whisk to avoid lumps as you slowly bring the sauce to the boil. Little by little, add the remaining stock. Reduce the heat and cook gently for another 30 minutes, stirring occasionally. Check that the sauce coats the back of the spoon before straining into a clean pan. If too thick, add a little more stock. If too thin, cook a little longer to reduce the sauce.
3 In a bowl, mix the egg yolks and cream. Stir in a little of the strained sauce, combine thoroughly and pour back into the pan. Stir to combine and warm gently to thicken the yolk. Do not boil. The sauce will separate if it overheats. Add the capers and season, to taste. Serve immediately with lamb.

Suprême sauce (top) and Caper sauce

Beurre fondu

This classic sauce can be varied by the liquid used to suit the dish with which it is served. It can be served with vegetables, chicken or fish. We have pictured it with a selection of vegetables.

*Preparation time **5–7 minutes***
*Total cooking time **10 minutes***
*Makes approximately **250 ml (8 fl oz)***

50 ml (1³/4 fl oz) water, dry white wine or chicken stock (see page 61)
200 g (6¹/2 oz) unsalted butter, cut into small cubes and chilled
lemon juice, to taste

1 Place the liquid (water, dry white wine or chicken stock) into a small saucepan and bring to the boil.
2 While the liquid is simmering, use an electic whisk to whisk in the cubes of butter, a few at a time, to obtain a smooth consistency. Remove the pan from the heat and season, to taste, with some lemon juice, salt and pepper. Serve the sauce immediately, or keep it warm (not hot), covered with plastic wrap, over a pan of warm water, for up to 30 minutes before use.

Chef's tip If the sauce becomes too cold, it will set. Warm it by stirring over a pan of hot water. If it becomes too hot, it will separate. Remove the bowl from the water and stir in a chip of ice or a few drops of cold water.

Beurre blanc

Another exquisite classic, seasoned with shallots, which is ideal to serve with fish such as the poached salmon cutlet shown in the picture.

*Preparation time **10 minutes***
*Total cooking time **25 minutes***
*Makes approximately **250 ml (8 fl oz)***

2 large French shallots, very finely chopped
100 ml (3¹/4 fl oz) white wine vinegar
100 ml (3¹/4 fl oz) dry white wine
200 g (6¹/2 oz) unsalted butter, cut into small cubes and chilled

1 Add the shallots, white wine vinegar and white wine to a small wide-based pan and heat over medium heat until the liquid has evaporated to 2 tablespoons.
2 As soon as the liquid boils, reduce the heat to very low and whisk in the butter, piece by piece. Whisk continuously to achieve a smooth and pale sauce. Season to taste with salt and pepper. Serve immediately, or transfer the sauce to a bowl, cover with plastic wrap and sit over a pan of warm water until ready to serve. You may wish to sieve the sauce for a smoother consistency. Serve with fish or chicken dishes.

Chef's tip Try adding a pinch of saffron threads with the wine. Also, try adding finely grated orange, lime or lemon rind or a small amount of chopped herbs such as tarragon, chives or dill.

Mousseline sauce

A simple but delicious sauce, shown here with steamed beans and poached white fish fillet.

Preparation time **15 minutes**
Total cooking time **5 minutes**
Makes approximately 500 ml (16 fl oz)

200 g (6¹/2 oz) clarified butter (see page 63)
3 egg yolks
small pinch of cayenne pepper, to taste
juice of ¹/2 lemon
30 ml (1 fl oz) cream, for whipping

1 Half fill a medium pan with water and heat until simmering. Have ready a heatproof bowl that will fit over the pan without actually touching the water.
2 To make the sauce, melt the butter in a separate pan. Place the egg yolks and 3 tablespoons water in the heatproof bowl and whisk until foamy. Place over the simmering water and whisk over low heat until thick and the mixture leaves a trail on the surface when the whisk is lifted. Remove from the heat and gradually add the melted butter, whisking constantly. When all the butter is incorporated, season with cayenne pepper, lemon juice and salt. Keep the sauce warm over the pan of warm water.
3 Half whip the cream until the trail made by the whisk can be seen, but if the bowl is tipped the cream just runs thickly. Add it to the sauce and fold very carefully. This sauce is excellent with poached fish or asparagus. Mousseline sauce is always served warm.

Chef's tip At no time must this sauce be allowed to get too hot or the yolks will cook and separate from the butter. To remedy, remove the pan from the water bath and try adding a few drops of cold water or a block of ice and whisking vigorously.

Béarnaise sauce

This creamy, tangy sauce is pictured with beef fillet, roast potatoes and baby cauliflower.

Preparation time **20 minutes**
Total cooking time **10 minutes**
Makes approximately 375 ml (12 fl oz)

260 g (8¹/4 oz) clarified butter (see page 63)
2 tablespoons fresh tarragon, roughly chopped
2 tablespoons fresh chervil, roughly chopped
1 French shallot, finely chopped
4 peppercorns, crushed roughly under a heavy pan
100 ml (3¹/4 fl oz) white wine vinegar
6 egg yolks
pinch of cayenne pepper

1 Half fill a medium pan with water and heat until simmering. Have ready a heatproof bowl that will fit over the pan without actually touching the water.
2 Melt the butter in a separate pan. Set aside 1 tablespoon tarragon and 1/2 tablespoon chervil. Place the shallots and peppercorns in a small saucepan with the vinegar and remaining tarragon and chervil. Bring to the boil and simmer for 4–6 minutes, or until the liquid has reduced by three quarters. Transfer to the heatproof bowl and place over the simmering water over very low heat. Add the egg yolks and whisk until thick and the mixture leaves a trail on the surface when the whisk is lifted.
3 Remove from the heat and gradually pour in the butter, whisking continuously, until all the butter is incorporated. Strain through a sieve and season with salt and cayenne pepper. Add the reserved tarragon and chervil just before serving. Serve lukewarm, don't overheat. If the sauce separates, whisk in a few drops of cold water or blocks of ice to restore consistency. The sauce may be kept warm in a clean bowl or small pan, covered with plastic wrap, and set over the pan of warm water.

Mousseline sauce (top) and Béarnaise sauce

Hollandaise sauce

This smooth, butter-based basic sauce is famed for serving with asparagus, as shown. See page 63 for step-by-step instructions to accompany this recipe.

*Preparation time **10 minutes***
*Total cooking time **10 minutes***
Makes approximately 500 ml (16 fl oz)

200 g (6¹/₂ oz) clarified butter (see page 63)
3 egg yolks, at room temperature
pinch of cayenne pepper (see Chef's tips)
1 teaspoon lemon juice

1 Half fill a pan with water and heat until simmering. Have ready a heatproof bowl that will fit over the pan without actually touching the water.

2 Melt the butter in a separate pan. Place the egg yolks and 3 tablespoons water in the heatproof bowl and whisk until foamy. Place over the simmering water and continue whisking over very low heat until thick and the mixture leaves a trail on the surface when the whisk is lifted. Gradually add the butter, whisking constantly. When all the butter is incorporated, strain the sauce into a clean pan or bowl and season with salt, to taste, cayenne pepper and lemon juice. Serve immediately, or keep the sauce warm by covering with plastic wrap and sitting over the pan of warm water.

Chef's tips If the sauce becomes too cold, it will set. Warm it by stirring over a pan of hot water. If it becomes too hot, it will separate. Remove the bowl from the water and stir in a block of ice or a few drops of cold water.

Measure out small amounts of cayenne pepper using the tip of a knife. Avoid using your fingertips as the residual pepper can cause discomfort if accidentally rubbed into the eyes or onto the lips.

Tomato sauce

This excellent tomato sauce, full of flavour, is shown here with deep-fried battered fish, but it would also be delicious served with meat or pasta.

*Preparation time **20 minutes***
*Total cooking time **45 minutes***
Makes approximately 410 ml (13 fl oz)

2 kg (4 lb) very ripe tomatoes or 4 x 425 g (13¹/2 oz)
  cans tomatoes, drained and roughly chopped
2 tablespoons olive oil
2 tablespoons tomato paste
100 g (3¹/4 oz) carrots, diced
100 g (3¹/4 oz) onions, diced
100 g (3¹/4 oz) bacon, diced
4 sprigs of fresh thyme
2 bay leaves
small pinch of cayenne pepper

1 If using fresh tomatoes, score a small cross in the bases, put in a bowl and cover with boiling water. Leave for 10 seconds before plunging into a bowl of iced water. Drain and, with the point of a sharp knife, remove the stalk and then peel, quarter and remove the seeds. Roughly chop the flesh.
2 Heat the olive oil in a pan over medium heat. Stir the tomato paste into the oil and cook for 30 seconds, stirring continuously with a wooden spoon to avoid burning. Stir in the carrot, onion and bacon and continue to cook gently, without colouring, for another 10 minutes, or until the vegetables are tender.
3 Add the tomato, thyme and bay leaves to the pan and gently cook for 30 minutes (longer if using canned tomatoes), stirring occasionally. Strain through a coarse sieve, pressing with a wooden spoon to extract as much liquid and pulp as possible. Discard the ingredients in the sieve. Season with salt and cayenne pepper and serve hot.

Apple sauce

The tartness of this sauce is the perfect accompaniment to roast pork, as pictured, and also for more fatty meats, such as duck or goose.

*Preparation time **15 minutes***
*Total cooking time **15 minutes***
Makes approximately 500 ml (16 fl oz)

4 medium-large cooking apples, peeled and cut
  into small cubes
pinch of cinnamon or cumin
2 teaspoons caster sugar

1 To make in a saucepan, combine the apple cubes, cinnamon or cumin and sugar in a pan and add enough water to barely cover the base of the pan. Cover with greaseproof paper and a lid and cook the apples over low-medium heat for 10–15 minutes, or until the apples have broken down to a purée. You may need to mash the apple with a fork or push it through a sieve to remove any lumps.
2 If a runnier consistency is required, add some water towards the end of cooking. Also, you may adjust the sweetness with more sugar to taste. Serve hot or cold.
3 To make in the microwave, place the apples in a large microwave-proof dish with the cinnamon or cumin and sugar. Microwave on High for about 4 minutes, or until the apples break down to a purée when pressed against the side of the dish with a fork.

Tomato sauce (top) and Apple sauce

Tomato coulis

A fresh tomato sauce that requires no cooking is perfect served in summer with chargrilled vegetables, such as the zucchini, eggplant and capsicum pictured, or, alternatively with savoury mousses.

Preparation time **20 minutes**
Total cooking time **Nil**
Makes approximately 650 ml (22 fl oz)

I kg (2 lb) very ripe tomatoes
I large French shallot, chopped
2 teaspoons olive oil
I tablespoon balsamic vinegar
2 tablespoons tomato paste, optional

1 Bring a pan of water to the boil. Meanwhile, cut a small cross in the bases of the tomatoes. Put them in a bowl, cover with boiling water and leave them for 10 seconds before plunging in a bowl of iced water. Drain and, with the point of a sharp knife, remove the stalk and then peel, quarter and remove the seeds. Roughly chop the flesh.
2 Blend the tomato and shallot in a blender until smooth. Pass them through a fine sieve and transfer to a round-based bowl.
3 Set the bowl on a tea towel to prevent it from moving while whisking. Gradually add the oil, in a thin steady stream, while whisking continuously. Once the mixture has emulsified or thickened, add the balsamic vinegar and season with salt and pepper. Alternatively, return the sieved tomato mixture to the blender and add the oil and vinegar as above. If the sauce does not have a shiny red colour or the tomato taste is very weak, whisk in the tomato paste to enhance both the colour and the taste.

Chef's tip When tomatoes are not in season, drained canned tomatoes could be used instead of fresh.

Red capsicum coulis

Use this coulis in the same way as a tomato coulis when a different flavour is required. It is shown here with grilled chicken kebabs.

Preparation time **10 minutes**
Total cooking time **25 minutes**
Makes approximately 220 ml (7 fl oz)

3 red capsicums (peppers)
20 g (³/4 oz) unsalted butter or I tablespoon olive oil
2 French shallots, finely chopped
I clove garlic, finely chopped
250 ml (8 fl oz) chicken or brown veal stock
  (see pages 60–61)

1 Cut the capsicums in half, remove the seeds and membrane, press the capsicums flat and lightly oil the skins. Cook under a preheated grill, skin-side-up, until the skin is evenly blistered and blackened. Remove, place in a plastic bag and when cool, peel away the skin and chop the flesh into even-sized pieces.
2 Heat the butter or oil in a heavy-based pan, add the shallot and garlic and cook gently for 1–2 minutes, without colouring, until softened. Add the capsicum, pour in 200 ml (6¹/2 fl oz) of the stock and bring to the boil. Reduce the heat and simmer for about 10 minutes until the liquid has reduced by half. Mash the soft capsicums against the sides of the pan to make a thick purée or work in a blender or food processor until smooth. Season, to taste, with salt and pepper.
3 Pass through a sieve and adjust the consistency with the remaining stock, if necessary. The coulis should coat the back of a spoon. Serve warm or chilled.

Chef's tip Use a stock to complement the dish it is intended to accompany, such as a fish stock for fish dishes, vegetable stock for vegetable dishes.

Tomato coulis (top) and Red capsicum coulis

Bread sauce

A classic accompaniment to roasted chicken, turkey or game, this delicately flavoured sauce is a favourite of the English. It is shown here with turkey and vegetables.

Preparation time **5 minutes + 15 minutes standing**
Total cooking time **15 minutes**
Makes approximately 400 ml (12³/₄ fl oz)

400 ml (12³/₄ fl oz) milk
8 cloves
1 small onion or 2 large French shallots
2 bay leaves
120 g (4 oz) fresh white breadcrumbs

1 Pour the milk into a saucepan and set over medium heat. Push the pointed end of the cloves into the onion and add the onion to the milk with the bay leaves. Bring slowly to the boil. Remove from the heat, cover and set aside for 15 minutes to allow the flavours to infuse into the milk.
2 Strain the milk through a fine sieve and discard the flavouring ingredients. Gradually add the breadcrumbs, whisking continuously, until the sauce has thickened to a thick pouring consistency. Season, to taste, with salt and pepper.
3 The sauce may be made a day in advance, although some additional milk should be added before serving as the breadcrumbs will have absorbed more milk overnight. Serve the sauce warm from a sauce boat.

Chef's tip You can also add a pinch of nutmeg or infuse the milk with other flavours such as peppercorns. Stir in a few raisins if serving the sauce with game. Stir in a little cream or a large nut of butter at the end for a richer sauce.

Rouille

This is the delicious traditional accompaniment for the bouillabaisse shown here.

Preparation time **20 minutes**
Total cooking time **1 hour 20 minutes**
Makes approximately 300 ml (10 fl oz)

1 medium floury potato
1 red capsicum (pepper)
1 egg yolk
1 teaspoon tomato paste
1 clove garlic, peeled
120 ml (4 fl oz) olive oil
pinch of cayenne

1 Preheat the oven to moderate 180°C (350°F/Gas 4). Set the potato on a baking tray and prick it several times with a fork. Bake for 1 hour, or until tender when tested with the point of a small knife. Alternatively, prick the potato all over, wrap in paper towel and microwave on High for 4–6 minutes, turning halfway through cooking. When cool enough to handle, cut in half and scoop out the flesh into a food processor.
2 Cut the capsicum in half and remove the seeds and membrane. Lightly oil the skin and cook under a preheated grill, skin-side-up, until the skin is blistered and blackened. Alternatively, bake for 15 minutes. Place in a plastic bag and when cool, peel away the skin. Add the flesh to the food processor with the egg yolk, tomato paste and garlic. Blend until smooth.
3 While the machine is running, gradually pour in the oil in a thin steady stream, until well incorporated. Season, to taste, with salt, pepper and cayenne pepper, remembering that the rouille should be quite fiery. Serve in a bowl or spread onto crisp bread croûtes. If serving as an accompaniment to a bouillabaisse, place a spoonful in the centre of the soup.

Bread sauce (top) and Rouille

Pesto

*This classic, uncooked basil, Parmesan and
pine nut sauce is traditionally served with
pasta, as pictured.*

Preparation time **15 minutes**
Total cooking time **Nil**
Makes approximately 800 ml (26 fl oz)

80 g (2³/4 oz) fresh basil
100 g (3¹/2 oz) Parmesan
2 cloves garlic, peeled
50 g (1³/4 oz) pine nuts
100 ml (3¹/4 fl oz) olive oil

1 Tear the basil leaves from the stalks, discarding the
stalks. Wash the basil leaves well and dry thoroughly in
a salad spinner or gently pat dry using a tea towel.
2 Grate the Parmesan, then process it in a food
processor until it resembles fine breadcrumbs. Add the
garlic and pine nuts and process briefly to roughly
combine the ingredients. Add the basil at this point and
process to combine.
3 While the machine is still running, slowly add the
olive oil until a paste is formed. Season, to taste, then
continue to add the oil until it reaches a spoonable
consistency. Serve the pesto stirred into spaghetti or
with chargrilled vegetables or meats. To store, cover and
leave in the refrigerator for up to 3 days.

Chef's tip If you wish to store the pesto for a longer
period, transfer it to a sterilised jar, cover the surface
with olive oil and store the jar in the refrigerator. Once
opened, the pesto must be used within 2–3 days.

Tomato concassé

*This is a classic vegetable preparation. The term
'concassé' is also used to describe finely diced tomato
used as a garnish. It is shown here with ravioli.*

Preparation time **15 minutes**
Total cooking time **15 minutes**
Makes approximately 250 ml (8 fl oz)

500 g (1 lb) ripe tomatoes
olive oil or good vegetable oil, for cooking
2 large French shallots, finely chopped
1 clove garlic, finely chopped
1 tablespoon tomato paste, optional
bouquet garni (see page 61)

1 Bring a pan of water to the boil. Meanwhile, cut a
small cross in the bases of the tomatoes. Put them in a
bowl, cover with boiling water and leave them for
10 seconds before plunging in a bowl of iced water.
Drain and, with the point of a sharp knife, remove the
stalk and then peel, quarter and remove the seeds.
Roughly chop the flesh.
2 Heat a little oil in a shallow pan and add the shallot
and garlic. Cook gently until softened, but not brown.
Stir in the tomato paste if the fresh tomatoes are not
particularly ripe.
3 Add the tomato to the pan with the bouquet garni
and cook rapidly, stirring continuously with a wooden
spoon, for about 7 minutes, or until the mixture is dry.
Remove the bouquet garni and season, to taste, with salt
and pepper.

Pesto (top) and Tomato concassé

Mango and coriander salsa

This tropical salsa is delicious served with grilled scallops or fish kebabs as pictured.

Preparation time **15 minutes + 30 minutes chilling**
Total cooking time **Nil**
Makes approximately 350 g (12 oz)

3 ripe mangoes
2 spring onions, finely chopped
3 tablespoons chopped fresh coriander
2 tablespoons lime juice, or to taste
finely chopped fresh ginger, to taste

1 Peel the skin from the mangoes, using a small paring knife. Slice down either side of the stone to release the flesh. Cut the flesh into even-sized cubes and place in a small bowl.

2 Add the spring onion and fresh coriander to the bowl and season with freshly ground black pepper. Stir to combine and add the lime juice and ginger, to taste. Cover the bowl with plastic wrap and chill in the refrigerator for 30 minutes before serving. Serve with cold meats, grilled fish or chicken dishes.

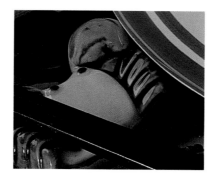

Sweet-and-sour sauce

This sauce, with a Chinese influence, goes extremely well with sautéed prawns, as shown here.

Preparation time **8 minutes**
Total cooking time **10 minutes**
Makes approximately 150 ml (5 fl oz)

1 1/2 **teaspoons cornflour**
3 tablespoons vinegar
2 tablespoons soft brown sugar
3 tablespoons pineapple juice
2 tablespoons tomato sauce
2 teaspoons soy sauce

1 Dissolve the cornflour in 11/2 teaspoons water and set aside. Add the remaining ingredients to a small saucepan and bring to the boil.
2 When the mixture is boiling, lower the heat, whisk in the combined cornflour and water and stir for about 5 minutes, or until thickened. Serve hot. This sauce goes well with deep-fried pork, sautéed prawns and chicken and can also be used as a dipping sauce.

Chinese lemon sauce

This is a classic Asian accompaniment for sautéed or deep-fried chicken strips. It also goes well with seafood and other poultry.

Preparation time **10 minutes**
Total cooking time **10 minutes**
Makes approximately 250 ml (8 fl oz)

60 ml (2 fl oz) lemon juice
60 ml (2 fl oz) chicken stock (see page 61)
1 tablespoon honey
1 tablespoon sugar
1/2 **teaspoon grated fresh ginger**
1 tablespoon cornflour
1–2 drops yellow food colouring

1 Put the lemon juice, stock, honey, sugar and ginger in a pan with 125 ml (4 fl oz) water. Stir over medium heat until the sugar dissolves.
2 Increase the heat and bring to the boil. Blend the cornflour with a little water and add to the pan, stirring constantly until the sauce boils and thickens. Remove from the heat, stir in the food colouring and season with a pinch of salt. Serve immediately.

Sweet-and-sour sauce (top) and Chinese lemon sauce

Salsa roja

Salsas are on the table at every meal in Mexico. There are over 100 different types of chilli and the hotness varies according to the particular chilli, the soil and the climate. Tortilla chips are shown here with the salsa.

*Preparation time **20 minutes + 2–3 hours refrigeration***
*Total cooking time **Nil***
Makes approximately 700 ml (23 fl oz)

3 ripe tomatoes, seeded and chopped
1 onion, chopped
3 Serrano chillies, seeded and chopped
2 teaspoons salt
2 teaspoons lime juice
1 tablespoon roughly chopped fresh coriander leaves

1 Stir all the ingredients in a bowl until well combined. Cover the bowl with plastic wrap and refrigerate for 2–3 hours to allow the flavours to mature.
2 You may serve this salsa chilled or at room temperature to accompany grilled fish, chicken, beef or as a dip with tortilla chips.

Chef's tips If you prefer a less chunky consistency, make the salsa in a food processor. Add the coriander at the end after the salsa has been roughly blended.
    Serrano chillies are medium to hot in flavour.

Peanut dipping sauce

This popular and versatile dipping sauce can be served with a variety of satay sticks, such as the skewered chicken shown, or with vegetables, such as broccoli florets, carrot or capsicum strips.

*Preparation time **10 minutes***
*Total cooking time **5 minutes***
Makes approximately 300 ml (10 fl oz)

125 g (4 oz) smooth peanut butter
1 clove garlic, finely chopped, optional
60 ml (2 fl oz) coconut milk
few drops of Tabasco, or to taste
1 tablespoon honey
1 tablespoon lemon juice
1 tablespoon light soy sauce

1 Combine the peanut butter, garlic, coconut milk and 60 ml (2 fl oz) water in a medium saucepan. Stir over medium heat for about 1–2 minutes, or until smooth and thick.
2 Add the Tabasco, honey, lemon juice and soy sauce and stir for about 1 minute, or until the sauce is warm and thoroughly combined.

Chef's tip Be careful not to overheat the sauce as it will separate easily.

Jus

A jus is made from the sticky caramelized juices left in the pan after roasting veal, poultry, lamb or beef. We have shown it with roast rack of lamb and steamed Asian greens.

Preparation time **15 minutes**
Total cooking time **30 minutes**
Makes approximately 250 ml (8 fl oz)

500 g (1 lb) roasted joint of meat or poultry
500 ml (16 fl oz) brown stock for dark meats or
  white stock for lighter meats (see pages 60–61)
1 carrot, chopped
1 onion, chopped
1 celery stick, chopped
1 leek, chopped
1 bay leaf
2 sprigs of fresh thyme
3 peppercorns

1 When the meat or poultry is cooked, remove it from the pan and allow to rest for 20 minutes. If there is a lot of fat in the pan, tip off most of it, leaving enough to fry the vegetables. In a separate pan, heat the stock over medium heat.

2 Add the carrot, onion, celery and leek to the roasting pan and cook gently on top of the stove for 5 minutes, stirring constantly with a wooden spoon to prevent burning, until golden brown. Tip the excess fat from the pan and add the bay leaf, thyme and peppercorns. Stir in some of the hot stock, scraping the base of the pan with a wooden spoon constantly until it boils.

3 Pour in the remaining stock and bring to the boil. Reduce the heat to a simmer and cook for about 5–10 minutes, or until reduced by half, skimming the surface of foam or fat throughout cooking. Strain the jus into a jug. Season, to taste, with salt and pepper.

Thickened roast gravy

This recipe can be made when roasting meats such as beef or chicken. It is shown with roast beef, Yorkshire pudding, roast potatoes and vegetables.

Preparation time **15 minutes**
Total cooking time **1–2 hours, depending on**
  meat chosen
Makes approximately 300 ml (10 fl oz)

oil, for cooking
meat of your choice, for roasting
1/2 onion, cut into large cubes
1 small carrot, cut into large cubes
1/2 celery stick, cut into large pieces
2 cloves garlic, lightly crushed
1 bay leaf
2 sprigs of fresh thyme
30 g (1 oz) plain flour
500 ml (16 fl oz) brown stock for dark meats or
  white stock for lighter meats (see pages 60–61)

1 Heat 5 mm (1/4 inch) of oil in a roasting pan on top of the stove. Add the meat and turn and baste for about 5 minutes to seal all sides. Remove the meat from the pan. Put the vegetables, garlic and herbs on the base of the pan. Lay the meat over the vegetables and roast at the temperature appropriate for the meat.

2 When the meat is cooked, remove and keep it warm. Drain off any fat, leaving the juices and sediment behind with the vegetables. If necessary, add more colour to the vegetables by frying on top of the stove in the roasting pan or returning to the oven.

3 Stir in the flour and cook for 1 minute over low heat. Remove from the heat and slowly add the stock, stirring to prevent lumps forming. Return to medium heat and stir until boiling. Lower the heat and simmer for 20 minutes, skimming froth and fat occasionally, then strain and season. Serve hot.

Bordelaise sauce

A sauce from the Bordeaux region of France, traditionally made with wine, shallots and bone marrow. The bone marrow in this particular recipe however is optional as the sauce is also delicious without it. It is pictured here with grilled steak.

Preparation time **10 minutes**
Total cooking time **20 minutes**
Makes approximately **250 ml (8 fl oz)**

300 g (10 oz) beef shin bone with marrow, cut into
  10 cm (4 inch) lengths, optional
4 French shallots, very finely chopped
6 peppercorns
1 sprig of fresh thyme
1/2 bay leaf
400 ml (12 3/4 fl oz) red wine
400 ml (12 3/4 fl oz) brown veal stock (see page 60)
15 g (1/2 oz) unsalted butter, cubed and chilled

1 If using the shin bone, prepare it by placing the pieces of bone in enough cold water to cover, then simmer for about 5 minutes, or until the marrow slips out easily. Thinly slice the marrow.
2 Place the shallots in a wide-based pan with the peppercorns, thyme and bay leaf. Stir in the red wine and bring to the boil. Reduce by simmering briskly for about 3 minutes, or until the liquid has evaporated and the pan is almost dry.
3 Stir in the veal stock, scraping the base of the pan with a wooden spoon, and return to the boil. Reduce the heat and simmer for 10 minutes, or until the sauce is reduced to 250 ml (8 fl oz). Skim the surface of the sauce occasionally. Season, to taste, with salt and pepper and skim the surface of the sauce again. Strain through a fine sieve before whisking in the butter, piece by piece, until the sauce has thickened slightly. Finish by adding the bone marrow, reheated by simmering in water or tossing in a hot pan. Serve hot.

Shellfish sauce

With similar ingredients to those used in a bisque, this sauce is perfect with all types of shellfish, especially lobster as shown.

Preparation time **20 minutes**
Total cooking time **1 hour**
Makes approximately **350 ml (11 fl oz)**

vegetable oil, for cooking
2 cloves garlic, lightly crushed
1/2 onion, roughly diced
1 small carrot, roughly diced
1 celery stick, chopped
1 bay leaf
2 sprigs of fresh thyme
500 g (1 lb) seafood shells such as crab, lobster
  or prawn shells
100 ml (3 1/4 fl oz) white wine
50 ml (1 3/4 fl oz) Cognac
30 g (1 oz) plain flour
2 tablespoons tomato paste
100 g (3 1/4 oz) tomatoes, stems removed, halved
  and seeded
1 litre fish stock (see page 61)
50 ml (1 3/4 fl oz) thick (double) cream, optional

1 Heat the oil and garlic gently in a large deep pan. Add the vegetables and cook, stirring occasionally, until the vegetables are soft and lightly coloured.
2 Stir in the bay leaf, thyme and shells. Pour in the wine and Cognac, scraping the base of the pan to lift all the juices. Cook until the pan is dry. Sprinkle the flour in and stir in the tomato paste and tomato. Add the stock and stir until boiling. Reduce the heat and simmer for 30–40 minutes, stirring occasionally.
3 Strain into a clean pan and keep warm. Season with salt and pepper and add the cream, if using. Serve hot.

Bordelaise sauce (top) and Shellfish sauce

Mayonnaise

Mayonnaise can be used as a sauce or a salad dressing. It is shown here with hard-boiled eggs, pumpernickel, olives, capers and gherkins. See page 62 for instructions to accompany this recipe.

Preparation time **10 minutes**
Total cooking time **Nil**
Makes approximately 400 ml (12³/4 fl oz)

2 egg yolks
50 g (1³/4 oz) Dijon mustard, or 1 heaped
 teaspoon dried mustard powder
275 ml (9 fl oz) peanut (groundnut) or olive oil
1 tablespoon white wine vinegar

1 Bring all the ingredients to room temperature. Set a large deep bowl on a tea towel to prevent it from moving. Add the egg yolks, mustard, ground white pepper, to taste, and 1 teaspoon salt, and mix well with a balloon whisk or with electric beaters.
2 Put the oil in a measuring cup or anything from which it is easy to pour. While whisking constantly or with the electric beaters operating, pour a thin stream of oil into the mixture. Begin with a small amount and stop beating periodically to allow each addition to emulsify to a thick, creamy mixture. Continue until 100 ml (3¹/4 fl oz) of oil has been added.
3 The mayonnaise should have begun to thicken well at this stage. Add the vinegar. The texture will thin slightly. Continue to add the remaining oil gradually.
4 Adjust the flavour of the mayonnaise with a touch more vinegar or salt and whisk in 1–2 tablespoons of boiling water if it curdles or separates.
5 The mayonnaise can be stored for up to a week in the refrigerator. Use it as a base for a number of sauces such as Thousand Island and tartare.

Thousand Island dressing

This creamy dressing is full of flavour and often served over a salad. Shown here with salad leaves and prawns, you could also use it in sandwiches or with burgers.

Preparation time **10 minutes + 20 minutes**
 refrigeration
Total cooking time **Nil**
Makes approximately 350 ml (11 fl oz)

250 g (8 oz) home-made or good-quality
 ready-made mayonnaise
80 g (2³/4 oz) tomato sauce
80 g (2³/4 oz) chilli relish or chilli sauce
1 small onion, grated
1 red or green capsicum (pepper), seeded and
 finely chopped
1 teaspoon Worcestershire sauce, or to taste
1 teaspoon Tabasco, or to taste
1 teaspoon brandy, or to taste

1 In a bowl, stir the mayonnaise, tomato sauce and chilli relish until combined. Stir in the onion, capsicum, Worcestershire sauce, Tabasco and brandy, each to taste.
2 Cover the bowl with plastic wrap and refrigerate until needed. Make the dressing at least 20 minutes ahead of serving and leave covered in the refrigerator to allow the flavours to develop.

Chef's tip Try serving this dressing on a crisp salad of iceberg lettuce. To turn the salad into a meal, add chilled cooked prawns and large garlicky croutons.

Mayonnaise (top) and Thousand Island dressing

Caesar salad dressing

Caesar salad is often thought of as an American dish, but was actually created by Caesar Cardini in Tijuana, Mexico in the 1920s.

Preparation time **10 minutes**
Total cooking time **Nil**
Makes approximately 250 ml (8 fl oz)

3 small cloves garlic, crushed
2 egg yolks
60 ml (2 fl oz) olive oil
1 teaspoon Worcestershire sauce
3 teaspoons lemon juice
55 g (1³/4 oz) Parmesan, grated

1 Using a balloon whisk or electric beaters, whisk the crushed garlic and egg yolks together in a large glass bowl. Start adding the olive oil, drop-by-drop or in a thin stream, whisking continuously until the dressing starts to thicken.
2 Add the Worcestershire sauce. Continue whisking in the remaining oil, lemon juice and finally the Parmesan.

Chef's tip To make a Caesar salad, toss washed and dried salad leaves in a large bowl with the dressing. Remove the crusts from four slices of bread and cut into small cubes. Fry in 30 ml (1 fl oz) olive oil until crisp and golden brown. Sprinkle the croutons over the salad leaves, then top with 45 g (1¹/2 oz) anchovy fillets and some grated Parmesan.

Sauce verte

This colourful, mayonnaise-based sauce complements dishes such as the poached salmon fillet shown here.

Preparation time **20 minutes**
Total cooking time **15 minutes**
Makes approximately 375 ml (12 fl oz)

50 g (1³/4 oz) English spinach leaves
50 g (1³/4 oz) fresh tarragon
I teaspoon chopped fresh chives
50 g (1³/4 oz) fresh chervil or parsley
50 g (1³/4 oz) watercress, trimmed
I clove garlic, roughly chopped
250 g (8 oz) home-made or good-quality ready-made mayonnaise

1 Wash the spinach leaves thoroughly three times in cold water until all traces of sand or dirt are removed. Drain. Wash the herbs thoroughly and drain.
2 Combine all the greenery in a food processor with the garlic and 30 ml (1 fl oz) water. Purée until fine.
3 Pour the mixture into a heavy-based pan, heat gently to simmering and cook until the mixture appears to be dry and looks slightly separated. Strain immediately through a muslin-lined sieve. Cool a little until you can draw the muslin ends together and twist to squeeze out any remaining moisture. Discard the liquid.
4 In a bowl, combine a small amount of the mayonnaise with the dry purée to loosen it. Add to the remainder of the mayonnaise to make a bright green sauce. Taste and season. Serve cold with salads, cold poached poultry and fish, soups and terrines.

Marie Rose sauce

Adjust the flavourings in this sauce to your own taste and serve with your favourite seafood, such as the grilled scallops and prawns pictured.

Preparation time **5 minutes**
Total cooking time **Nil**
Makes approximately 350 ml (11 fl oz)

250 g (8 oz) home-made or good-quality ready-made mayonnaise
80 g (2³/4 oz) tomato sauce
Worcestershire sauce, to taste
Tabasco, to taste
brandy, to taste

1 Stir the mayonnaise and tomato sauce together in a small bowl. Add a few drops each of Worcestershire sauce, Tabasco and brandy and stir to combine.
2 Cover the sauce with plastic wrap and chill in the refrigerator. Serve with seafood.

Sauce verte (top) and Marie Rose sauce

Tartare sauce

Add capers and gherkins to mayonnaise for a sauce that teams perfectly with deep-fried battered fish, as pictured here.

Preparation time **10 minutes + 30 minutes refrigeration**
Total cooking time **Nil**
Makes approximately 350 ml (11 fl oz)

25 g (³/4 oz) capers, drained and finely chopped
50 g (1³/4 oz) small gherkins, drained and finely chopped
250 g (8 oz) home-made or good-quality ready-made mayonnaise
1 tablespoon chopped fresh parsley, or to taste

1 In a small bowl, mix the capers and gherkins with the mayonnaise. Add the parsley, to your own taste.
2 You may serve the sauce immediately or cover with plastic wrap and chill in the refrigerator for 30 minutes before serving. Serve with grilled or fried fish.

Chef's tip You could try adding lemon juice, finely diced French shallot or chopped chives, to taste.

Andalouse sauce

A hint of sweetness and colour to complement seafood, such as the pan-fried fish shown here with braised baby fennel.

Preparation time **5 minutes + 30 minutes refrigeration**
Total cooking time **Nil**
Makes approximately 350 ml (11 fl oz)

30 g (1 oz) bottled or canned red pimiento
250 g (8 oz) home-made or good-quality ready-made mayonnaise
80 g (2³/4 oz) tomato sauce

1 Drain the pimiento, finely dice and set aside. Place the mayonnaise in a small bowl and stir in the tomato sauce until well combined. Mix in the pimiento.
2 Cover the sauce with plastic wrap and chill in the refrigerator for 30 minutes before serving. Serve with grilled or fried fish or as a dip.

Tartare sauce (top) and Andalouse sauce

Rémoulade sauce

This sauce, which is the traditional accompaniment to grated celeriac, is also delicious with cold meats such as the ham, turkey and beef pictured here.

*Preparation time **10 minutes + 10 minutes refrigeration + 15 minutes soaking***
*Total cooking time **Nil***
Makes approximately 325 ml (10¹/₄ fl oz)

3 anchovy fillets
60 ml (2 fl oz) milk
250 g (8 oz) home-made or good-quality
  ready-made mayonnaise
2 teaspoons Dijon mustard
25 g (³/₄ oz) capers, drained and chopped
50 g (1³/₄ oz) gherkins, drained and chopped

1 Place the anchovy fillets in a small bowl, soak in the milk for 15 minutes, then drain. Discard the milk and finely chop the anchovies.
2 Stir the mayonnaise in a small bowl with the chopped anchovies and mustard until combined. Mix the capers and the gherkins into the sauce.
3 Cover with plastic wrap and place in the refrigerator to chill for 10 minutes, or until required for serving. Serve the rémoulade sauce with grilled fish, grated celeriac or cold meats.

Classic vinaigrette

A classic vinaigrette may be used to add a tang to all types of salads or vegetables. Here it is shown simply with mixed salad leaves.

*Preparation time **5 minutes***
*Total cooking time **Nil***
Makes approximately 250 ml (8 fl oz)

2 tablespoons Dijon mustard
50 ml (1³/₄ fl oz) white wine vinegar
200 ml (6¹/₂ fl oz) olive oil or good-quality salad oil

1 Whisk together the mustard and vinegar in a bowl, with salt and pepper, to taste.
2 Slowly drizzle in the oil, whisking continuously. This will result in an emulsification, giving a thick smooth texture, rather than the oil separating and sitting on top. If the vinaigrette is too sharp for your taste, add a little more oil.
3 The vinaigrette may be kept at room temperature, in a sealed container and out of direct sunlight, for up to 1 week before serving.

Chef's tip As a rule of thumb, the guide for vinaigrettes is one part acid (wine vinegar or lemon juice) to four parts oil.

Rémoulade sauce (top) and Classic vinaigrette

Raspberry vinaigrette

This delicious vinaigrette is shown served with avocado and green salad leaves.

Preparation time **10 minutes**
Total cooking time **Nil**
Makes approximately 250 ml (8 fl oz)

100 g (3¼ oz) raspberries, fresh or frozen
50 ml (1¾ fl oz) white wine vinegar
1 tablespoon sugar, or to taste
200 ml (6½ fl oz) corn oil or good-quality salad oil

1 Process the raspberries and the vinegar in a blender or food processor until a smooth purée is formed. If the raspberries are quite sharp or out of season, you may add the sugar at this stage.

2 While the blender is still operating, gradually add the oil in a thin stream. Season the vinaigrette, to taste, with salt and pepper and then strain through a fine sieve to remove the seeds. The vinaigrette can be served immediately or covered and kept in the refrigerator for up to 48 hours, though the colour will be dulled a little by storage.

Gribiche sauce

*Particularly good to liven up mild foods.
Try serving this sauce with vegetables,
such as artichokes or white asparagus.*

Preparation time **10 minutes**
Total cooking time **Nil**
Makes approximately 275 ml (8³/4 fl oz)

250 ml (8 fl oz) vinaigrette (see page 44)
¹/2 tablespoon chopped gherkins
¹/2 tablespoon chopped capers
¹/2 tablespoon chopped spring onion
¹/2 hard-boiled egg, sieved

1 Stir the vinaigrette, gherkins, capers, spring onions and egg in a bowl until combined. Season, to taste, with salt and pepper.
2 You may serve the sauce immediately or cover with plastic wrap and refrigerate for up to 24 hours.

Chef's tips Sieve the egg through a stainless metal sieve, a nylon sieve is too soft and you will find it difficult to push through.

Serve with fish dishes such as poached trout or bass, or cooked artichoke bottoms or hearts.

Cucumber vinaigrette

*An interesting variation on a classic vinaigrette.
Delicious served with smoked trout as pictured here.*

Preparation time **15 minutes**
Total cooking time **5 minutes**
Makes approximately 250 ml (8 fl oz)

¹/2 cucumber, about 100 g (3¹/4 oz)
3 teaspoons white wine vinegar
3 teaspoons Dijon mustard
100 ml (3¹/4 fl oz) light salad oil, such as
  corn or peanut (groundnut)

1 Fill a small pan with salted water and bring to the boil. Peel the cucumber and reserve both the flesh and the peel. Remove and discard the cucumber seeds. Add the peel to the water, return to the boil and lower the heat to simmer until just tender. Drain the peel and place in a bowl of iced water for 10 seconds, then drain. Process the skin in a blender with the vinegar and mustard until it forms a smooth purée.
2 While the blender is running, gradually add the oil in a thin steady stream. Add the cucumber flesh and continue to a purée. Season with salt and pepper, to taste. Strain if a smoother texture is required. This vinaigrette may be refrigerated, covered with plastic wrap, for up to 2 days, but ideally should be served within 1–2 hours.

Gribiche sauce (top) and Cucumber vinaigrette

Citrus fruit vinaigrette

This dressing is well suited to being served with a salad to accompany goose, pork or Chinese duck as shown in the picture.

Preparation time **15 minutes + 1–2 hours standing**
Total cooking time **Nil**
Makes approximately 500 ml (16 fl oz)

juice and finely grated rind of 1 orange
juice and finely grated rind of 1 lemon
juice and finely grated rind of 1/2 grapefruit
300 ml (10 fl oz) corn oil or other good-quality salad oil

1 Place the rinds and fruit juices in a bowl. Gradually whisk the oil into the mixture and season, to taste, with salt and pepper. This can be done in a blender.
2 Cover with plastic wrap and leave at room temperature for 1–2 hours to allow the flavours to mature before serving.

Chef's tip The quantity of oil may be decreased or increased depending on the size of the fruit and according to personal taste.

Vinaigrette à l'ancienne

This dressing derives its name from the wholegrain mustard used, known as 'moutarde à l'ancienne' in French. It is shown here with a potato and chive salad.

Preparation time **5 minutes**
Total cooking time **Nil**
Makes approximately 300 ml (10 fl oz)

1 tablespoon wholegrain mustard
50 ml (13/4 fl oz) white wine vinegar
200 ml (61/2 fl oz) good-quality salad oil

1 Place the mustard and vinegar in a bowl with salt and pepper, to taste, and whisk together.
2 Sit the bowl on a tea towel to prevent it from moving while adding the oil. Gradually add the oil, pouring it in a thin steady stream, while whisking continuously. This will prevent the vinegar and oil separating.

Chef's tip The amount of oil used will alter the piquancy and thickness of the dressing. Less oil in the recipe will produce a sharper taste and thinner texture.

Blue cheese dressing

Very versatile, this all-time favourite dressing may be served with either vegetables, pears or avocado as shown here.

Preparation time **15 minutes**
Total cooking time **Nil**
Makes approximately 350 ml (11 fl oz)

80 g (2³/4 oz) crumbly blue cheese,
  (Roquefort or Stilton are ideal)
80 ml (2³/4 fl oz) white wine vinegar
160 ml (5¹/4 fl oz) light olive oil
50 g (1³/4 oz) fresh parsley, finely chopped

1 In a small glass bowl, crumble the blue cheese and mash it to a smooth paste with a fork.
2 To make a vinaigrette, in a separate bowl, whisk together the vinegar and salt and pepper, to taste. While whisking, gradually add the oil in a thin steady stream until the mixture is thick and smooth, i.e. emulsified.
3 Pour the vinaigrette over the cheese and add the chopped parsley. Stir the mixture until the dressing is smooth but retains some of the cheese chunks. Adjust the flavour with salt and pepper if necessary. Serve with avocado, pieces of raw fruit or vegetable to dip in, and green salads.

Dill sauce

This slightly sweet sauce is the popular accompaniment to Scandinavian gravlax, as shown here, or any other smoked fish.

Preparation time **10 minutes**
Total cooking time **Nil**
Makes approximately 150 ml (5 fl oz)

I heaped teaspoon wholegrain mustard
I heaped tablespoon Dijon mustard
¹/2 teaspoon sugar
75 ml (2¹/2 fl oz) peanut (groundnut) oil
I tablespoon white wine vinegar
I tablespoon chopped fresh dill

1 Sit a large glass bowl on a folded tea towel to prevent it from moving. Whisk the wholegrain mustard, Dijon, sugar and a pinch of salt in the bowl until well blended.
2 Pour the oil into the mixture in a very fine steady stream while whisking constantly. It is easier to pour the oil if you place it in a jug with a pouring lip. Continue until the mixture has thickened and approximately half the oil has been added. Slowly add all the vinegar while still whisking and finally, continue until all the oil has been added and the mixture has emulsified smoothly.
3 Stir in the chopped dill and add 1 tablespoon of hot water (this is a safety measure which helps to prevent the emulsified sauce from separating).

Blue cheese dressing (top) and Dill sauce

Crème anglaise

A rich custard sauce, with a light consistency that is traditionally flavoured with vanilla. Serve hot or cold to accompany all types of desserts, such as the poached peach shown in the picture. See page 63 for additional instructions to accompany this recipe.

Preparation time **5 minutes**
Total cooking time **20 minutes**
Makes approximately 350 ml (11 fl oz)

250 ml (8 fl oz) milk
I vanilla pod, split lengthways
3 egg yolks
30 g (I oz) caster sugar

1 Pour the milk into a deep, heavy-based saucepan over medium heat. Scrape the seeds from the vanilla pod and add to the milk with the pod. Slowly bring to the boil to allow the flavour of the vanilla to infuse into the milk. Remove from the heat.

2 In a bowl, using a wooden spoon, whisk together the egg yolks and the sugar until pale and thick. Pour the hot milk onto the yolks and mix well. Pour the mixture back into a clean saucepan and cook over extremely gentle heat, stirring continuously, for 5 minutes, or until it begins to thicken and coats the back of a spoon. If the mixture is getting too hot, remove the pan from the heat for a few seconds and continue to stir. Do not allow it to boil. Strain into a bowl and discard the vanilla pod. If serving cold, allow the custard to cool before chilling in the refrigerator. To reheat the sauce, transfer to a heatproof bowl or deep dish and set over a pan of hand-hot water, stirring continuously and taking care not to overheat.

Chef's tips This custard sauce can be kept in the refrigerator for up to 3 days in a sealed container.

Take extra care when cooking the basic mixture. If the heat is too high, the mixture will cook too quickly around the sides of the pan and curdle or separate as the egg yolks become overcooked and 'scramble' in the milk. The sauce may be saved by adding a dash of cold milk and rapidly whisking, which releases the heat as quickly as possible to reduce any further curdling. If the sauce has curdled and been saved in this way, it may be slightly lumpy and need to be passed through a sieve before using.

Variations

Flavour the sauce using an alcohol, liqueur or coffee essence, or add 2 drops of vanilla essence to the egg yolks instead of the vanilla pod.

PISTACHIO CREAM
Stir in 1 tablespoon pistachio paste, or chopped pistachios that have been puréed in a food processor or ground to a paste using a mortar and pestle. Stir the paste into the cream while warm.

COFFEE CREAM
Dissolve 1 tablespoon instant coffee in 1 teaspoon hot water, kahlua or crème de caçao and stir into the warm cream. You could also use espresso or strong coffee.

CHESTNUT CREAM
Stir in 1 tablespoon of sweetened chestnut purée. In this case, cut down the sugar in the crème anglaise basic mixture to 20 g (3/4 oz).

Chocolate sauce

*A delightful accompaniment for many desserts and
fruits, such as the poached pear and vanilla
ice cream shown here.*

Preparation time **10 minutes**
Total cooking time **20 minutes**
Makes approximately 315 ml (10 fl oz)

225 g (7¼ oz) caster sugar
100 g (3¼ oz) dark chocolate, chopped
25 g (¾ oz) good-quality cocoa powder, sifted

1 Combine 300 ml (10 fl oz) of water with the sugar
and chopped chocolate in a medium saucepan and
slowly bring to the boil, stirring continuously. Remove
from the heat.
2 In a bowl, mix the cocoa powder and 50 ml (1¾ fl oz)
water to a smooth paste. Pour this into the saucepan
over medium heat and bring back to the boil, whisking
vigorously and continuously. Simmer, uncovered, for
5–10 minutes, until the sauce coats the back of a spoon.
Do not allow the sauce to boil over. Strain and allow to
cool a little.

Chef's tip This sauce may be served hot or cold and
keeps well for up to 1 week if stored in an airtight
container in the refrigerator.

Butterscotch sauce

*A very rich sauce ideal to serve hot with ice cream.
It also works particularly well with waffles.*

Preparation time **5 minutes**
Total cooking time **15 minutes**
Makes approximately 315 ml (10 fl oz)

1 vanilla pod, split lengthways
450 ml (14¼ fl oz) cream
200 g (6½ oz) caster sugar

1 Scrape the seeds from the vanilla pod and add with
the pod to a saucepan with the cream. Bring slowly to
the boil, remove from the heat and allow the flavours
to infuse into the cream, then strain and discard the
vanilla pod.
2 In a separate saucepan and using a wooden spoon,
stir half the sugar continuously over medium heat, until
the sugar has melted. Add the remaining sugar and
cook until the sugar is fluid and light golden.
3 Remove from the heat and add the cream in a slow
steady stream, stirring continuously. Be careful as the
sugar will splatter when the liquid is added. When all
the cream has been incorporated, return to the boil and
cook, stirring, until the sauce coats the back of the
spoon. If you have a few lumps of sugar left in the
bottom of the pan simply pass the liquid through a wire
sieve. This sauce may be served either hot or cold.

Chef's tip For an adult version of the sauce, try adding
a little malt whisky, to taste. You could also add a little
espresso coffee, to taste.

Chocolate sauce (top) and Butterscotch sauce

Fruit coulis

Make this fabulous fruit sauce using any berries in season. Ideal for serving with any dessert, ice cream or sorbet.

Preparation time **5 minutes**
Total cooking time **5 minutes**
Makes approximately 250 ml (8 fl oz)

250 g (8 oz) firm ripe raspberries
125 g (4 oz) caster sugar
juice of 1/2 lemon
alcohol or liqueur of your choice

1 Prepare the fruit by picking over and removing any bruised or overripe fruit.

2 Combine the raspberries in a medium saucepan with the caster sugar and lemon juice and bring to the boil to soften the berries slightly. Remove from the heat and allow to cool.

3 Transfer to a food processor and blend to a smooth purée. Pass through a fine sieve to remove the seeds. At this stage your favourite alcohol can be added, to taste. This sauce can be kept in a covered container in the refrigerator for up to 1 week and should be served cold.

Chef's tips Try Kirsch, Calvados, eau de vie de poivre, or Cointreau.

When fresh berries are not available, use frozen ones instead. Thaw them before use. You may need to adjust the sugar content accordingly.

A quick, non-cook method if the fruit is very soft and will purée easily is to process with icing sugar instead of caster sugar, sieve and then add the lemon juice.

Orange and Grand Marnier sauce

Crepes or ice cream can be dressed up with this sophisticated tangy sauce.

Preparation time **10–15 minutes**
Total cooking time **20 minutes**
Makes approximately 300 ml (10 fl oz)

250 ml (8 fl oz) fresh orange juice
25 g (3/4 oz) sugar
I teaspoon finely grated orange rind
200 g (61/2 oz) unsalted butter, cut into small cubes and chilled
60 ml (2 fl oz) Grand Marnier, Cognac or Cointreau

1 Bring the orange juice, sugar and orange rind slowly to the boil in a saucepan. Continue to boil, stirring occasionally, until the liquid becomes syrupy.

2 Whisk the butter into the boiling liquid, piece by piece, until a smooth consistency is obtained. Remove the pan from the heat and add the liqueur, to taste. Serve the sauce immediately or keep it warm (not hot) for no more than about 30 minutes before use.

Chef's tip If the sauce becomes too cold, it will set. If it is too hot, it will separate. To rescue the sauce from both problems, melt the former to a lukewarm heat and cool the latter to the same temperature. You can do this by bringing to the boil a small amount of water or orange juice, then whisking in a small amount of hard butter to obtain a smooth consistency. Slowly add either of the problem sauces to this mixture, whisking continuously.

Fruit coulis (top) and Orange and Grand Marnier sauce

Chef's techniques

◆

Making brown stock

Roasting the bones gives a good colour to the stock and helps to remove the excess fat.

Roast 1.5 kg (3 lb) beef or veal bones at very hot 230°C (450°F/Gas 8) for 40 minutes, adding a quartered onion, 2 chopped carrots, 1 chopped leek and 1 chopped celery stick halfway through.

Transfer to a clean pan. Add 4 litres water, 2 tablespoons tomato paste, bouquet garni and 6 peppercorns. Simmer for 3–4 hours, skimming often.

Ladle the stock in batches into a fine sieve over a bowl. Gently press the solids with the ladle to extract all the liquid and place in the refrigerator to cool. Lift off any solidified fat. Makes 1.5–2 litres.

Making lamb stock

Ask your butcher to chop the lamb bones so they will fit in your saucepan.

Put 1.5 kg (3 lb) of lamb bones in a large stockpot. Cover with water and bring to the boil. Drain and rinse the bones.

Return the bones to a clean saucepan and add 1 quartered onion, 2 carrots, 1 leek and 1 celery stick, all chopped, as well as 3 litres of water, 1 bouquet garni and 6 peppercorns.

Bring to the boil, reduce the heat and simmer for 2–3 hours, skimming the fat and scum from the surface regularly. A flat strainer is easiest to use for skimming.

Ladle the bones and vegetables into a fine sieve over a bowl. Press the bones and vegetables with the ladle to extract all the liquid. Refrigerate for several hours and remove the solidified fat. Makes about 1.5 litres.

Making chicken stock

*Good, flavoursome home-made stock
can be the cornerstone of a great dish.*

Cut up 750 g (1 1/2 lb) chicken bones and carcass and put in a pan with a roughly chopped onion, carrot and celery stick. Add 6 peppercorns, a bouquet garni and 4 litres cold water.

Bring to the boil and let the stock simmer gently for 2–3 hours, skimming off any scum that rises to the surface using a large spoon. Strain the stock through a sieve into a clean bowl, then allow to cool.

Chill the stock overnight, then lift off any fat. If you can't leave overnight, drag the surface of the hot strained stock with paper towels to lift off the fat. Makes 1.5–2 litres.

Making fish stock

*Use white fish, rather than oily fish such as salmon,
trout or mackerel. Remove the eyes and gills.*

Place 2 kg (4 lb) chopped fish bones and trimmings in salted water for 10 minutes; drain. Return to a clean pan with 2.5 litres water, 12 peppercorns, 2 bay leaves, chopped celery stick and onion and juice of 1 lemon.

Bring to the boil, then reduce the heat and simmer for 20 minutes. During simmering, skim off any scum that rises to the surface using a large spoon.

Ladle the stock in batches into a fine sieve over a bowl. Gently press the solids with a ladle to extract all the liquid and place in the refrigerator to cool. Makes 1.5 litres.

Freezing stock cubes

*Stock will keep in the refrigerator for 3 days. It can
be frozen in portions for later use, for 6 months.*

After removing any fat, boil the stock until reduced to 500 ml (16 fl oz). Cool and freeze until solid. Transfer to a plastic bag and seal. To make 2 litres stock, add 1.5 litres water to 500 ml (16 fl oz) concentrated stock.

Bouquet garni

*Add the flavour and aroma of herbs to your
dish with a freshly made bouquet garni.*

Wrap the green part of a leek loosely around a bay leaf, a sprig of thyme, some celery leaves and a few stalks of parsley, then tie with string. Leave a long tail to the string for easy removal.

White sauce

Flour and butter are cooked to make a roux to thicken white sauce.

Add the flour to melted butter in a saucepan over low heat. Stir with a wooden spoon.

Cook the flour mixture over the heat for 1–2 minutes, without browning, to create a roux.

Remove from the heat and gradually add the milk to the roux, beating until smooth.

Return to medium heat and bring to the boil, stirring constantly. Cook until the mixture thickens and coats the back of the spoon.

Mayonnaise

To make a successful mayonnaise, have all the ingredients at the same temperature.

Stand a large, deep bowl on a tea towel to make it stable. Whisk the egg yolks, mustard, white pepper and salt in the bowl until evenly combined.

To begin with, whisk in a thin stream of oil until the mixture thickens. If the oil is added too quickly, the mayonnaise will separate.

After the first 100 ml (3 1/4 fl oz) of oil has been added, whisk in the vinegar. Add the remaining oil gradually.

Hollandaise sauce

This sauce must not be allowed to get too hot, otherwise it may curdle.

Whisk the egg yolks and water together in a medium bowl until foamy. Place the bowl into a large shallow pan half-filled with hot water. Gradually whisk in the butter.

Continue adding the butter, whisking constantly. The sauce should leave a trail on the surface when the whisk is lifted.

Once all the butter is incorporated, strain the sauce into a clean bowl and then season, to taste.

Clarifying butter

Removing the water and solids from butter makes it less likely to burn. Ghee is a form of clarified butter.

To make 100 g (3^1/4 oz) clarified butter, cut 180 g (5^3/4 oz) butter into small cubes. Place in a small pan set into a larger pot of water over low heat. Melt the butter without stirring.

Remove the pan from the heat and allow to cool slightly. Skim the foam from the surface, being careful not to stir the butter.

Pour off the clear yellow liquid, being very careful to leave the milky sediment behind in the pan. Discard the sediment and store the clarified butter in an airtight container in the refrigerator.

Making crème anglaise

When making an egg custard sauce, keep the heat gentle and stir constantly to prevent scorching.

Stir the custard constantly over very gentle heat until the sauce thickens. Test the consistency by running your finger through the custard along the back of a wooden spoon. It should leave a clear line.

Published in 1998 by Merehurst Limited, Ferry House, 51–57 Lacy Road, Putney, London SW15 1PR.

Merehurst Limited, Murdoch Books and Le Cordon Bleu thank the 32 masterchefs of all the Le Cordon Bleu Schools, whose knowledge and expertise have made this book possible, especially: Chef Cliche (MOF), Chef Terrien, Chef Boucheret, Chef Duchêne (MOF), Chef Guillut, Chef Steneck, Paris; Chef Males, Chef Walsh, Chef Hardy, London; Chef Chantefort, Chef Bertin, Chef Jambert, Chef Honda, Tokyo; Chef Salembien, Chef Boutin, Chef Harris, Sydney; Chef Lawes, Adelaide; Chef Guiet, Chef Denis, Ottawa. Of the many students who helped the Chefs test each recipe, a special mention to graduates David Welch and Allen Wertheim. A very special acknowledgment to Directors Susan Eckstein, Great Britain, and Kathy Shaw, Paris, who have been responsible for the coordination of the Le Cordon Bleu team throughout this series.

Managing Editor: Kay Halsey
Series Concept, Design and Art Direction: Juliet Cohen
Editor: Wendy Stephen
Food Director: Jody Vassallo
Food Editors: Dimitra Stais, Tracy Rutherford
Designer: Annette Fitzgerald
Photographers: Chris Jones, Jon Bader
Food Stylists: Mary Harris, Amanda Cooper
Food Preparation: Michelle Earl, Kerrie Mullins, Michelle Lawton
Chef's Techniques Photographer: Reg Morrison
Home Economists: Anna Beaumont, Michelle Earl, Michelle Lawton, Kerrie Mullins, Justine Poole, Kerrie Ray, Alison Turner

Creative Director: Marylouise Brammer
International Sales Director: Mark Newman
CEO & Publisher: Anne Wilson

ISBN 1 85391 780 X

Printed by Toppan Printing (S) Pte Ltd
First Printed 1998
©Design and photography Murdoch Books® 1998
©Text Le Cordon Bleu 1998
All rights reserved. No part of this publication may be reproduced, stored in a retrieval system or transmitted in any form or by any means, electronic, mechanical, photocopying, recording or otherwise without the prior written permission of the publisher.

A catalogue record for this book is available from the British Library.

Distributed in the UK by D Services, 6 Euston Street, Freemen's Common, Leicester LE2 7SS Tel 0116-254-7671 Fax 0116-254-4670.
Distributed in Canada by Whitecap (Vancouver) Ltd, 351 Lynn Avenue, North Vancouver, BC V7J 2C4 Tel 604-980-9852 Fax 604-980-8197 or Whitecap (Ontario) Ltd, 47 Coldwater Road, North York, ON M3B 1Y8 Tel 416-444-3442 Fax 416-444-6630
Published and distributed in Australia by Murdoch Books®, 45 Jones Street, Ultimo NSW 2007

The Publisher and Le Cordon Bleu wish to thank Carole Sweetnam for her help with this series and Villeroy & Boch for their assistance with the photography..
Front cover: Hollandaise sauce shown with asparagus.

IMPORTANT INFORMATION

CONVERSION GUIDE

1 cup = 250 ml (8 fl oz)
1 Australian tablespoon = 20 ml (4 teaspoons)
1 UK tablespoon = 15 ml (3 teaspoons)

NOTE: We have used 20 ml tablespoons. If you are using a 15 ml tablespoon, for most recipes the difference will be negligible. For recipes using baking powder, gelatine, bicarbonate of soda and flour, add an extra teaspoon for each tablespoon specified.

CUP CONVERSIONS—DRY INGREDIENTS

1 cup flour, plain or self-raising = 125 g (4 oz)
1 cup sugar, caster = 250 g (8 oz)
1 cup breadcrumbs, dry = 125 g (4 oz)

IMPORTANT: Those who might be at risk from the effects of salmonella food poisoning (the elderly, pregnant women, young children and those suffering from immune deficiency diseases) should consult their GP with any concerns about eating raw eggs.